MW00681846

Science is Childsplay

Terry Cash

Illustrations by Eira Reeves

Longman

LONGMAN GROUP UK LIMITED

Longman House
Burnt Mill, Harlow, Essex CM20 2JE, England
and Associated Companies throughout the World

© Terry Cash 1989

All rights reserved. No part of this publication
may be reproduced, stored in a retrieval system,
or transmitted in any form or by any means, electronic,
mechanical, photocopying, recording or otherwise,
without the prior written permission of the copyright
owner.

The illustrations are by Eira Reeves

First published 1989

British Library Cataloguing in Publication Data

Cash, Terry
    Science is child's play.
    1. Science. Experiments
I. Title.   II. Series
    507'.24

ISBN 0-582-03627-5

Set in 11/12pt Frutiger 45 Light, Linotron 202

Produced by Longman Group (FE) Ltd
Printed in Hong Kong

Contents

Energy 36

Forces 51

Introduction

Never before has science been so important in schools and an understanding of scientific things so important to our children.

Although many Primary Schools have included some science in their work for many years, for the first time it is now a requirement that all schools should introduce even the youngest pupils to a wide variety of science related activities and processes.

This book is for the concerned parent who would like her child to have a head start along this important road. With step by step instructions it guides the reader through simple, but essential activities that will lay the foundations for a clear understanding of basic scientific processes and, more importantly, the feeling of fun and fulfilment that science can offer the prepared mind.

No previous knowledge of science is required or expected on the part of the parent, just a willingness to help your child in their discoveries and to learn together.

Many of the activities begin with background information for the parent which explains the scientific aspects concerned. There is also a comprehensive list of items required to enable your child to tackle each task. However, it is fully appreciated that expensive items are not easily obtainable, so most of the experiments and investigations can be attempted with nothing more than items of household junk. In fact the only thing that is needed is a sense of curiosity and inquisitiveness that every child has as a natural gift . . . happy experimenting!

 # e and my world

OURSELVES

What better place to begin than with ourselves? This section will help your child come to understand what a wonderful creation the human body is and to appreciate the countless skills and abilities that we possess.

How tall am I?

Children like to know how tall they are and by how much they have grown. If it is possible, keep a permanent record of your child's height in a suitable spot at home. This could be on a door frame or stair post or just a paper strip taped to the wall. Use a pen that won't fade or wipe off to mark and date your child's height every three months.

It is not necessary to do so, but if you have a ruler or tape measure you can measure your child's actual height.

Although we generally give our height in feet and inches, measure your child in centimetres too, so that she gets used to recognising her own height in metric units. (These are often used by shops for children's clothing sizes.)

It is amazing how quickly young children grow, but, if you continue keeping the record for a few years, you will also notice that the growth isn't always regular. Sometimes there can be quite a period of limited growth, then all of a sudden they shoot up.

What do I weigh?

Interest in weight goes hand in hand with height. If you intend to keep a record of height as suggested, then your child's weight can be made part of that record at the same time.

Once again, although we tend to quote our weight as stones and pounds, it is useful to use bathroom scales that give the metric equivalent in kilogrammes as well.

It is surprising how a child's weight can remain relatively stable even during periods of considerable growth and then rise on other occasions without apparent reason.

Body pictures

Another way to make a record of your child's overall size is to lay her down on a large sheet of paper, lengths of old wallpaper taped together will do very well. Now draw round her and help her to cut out her shape.

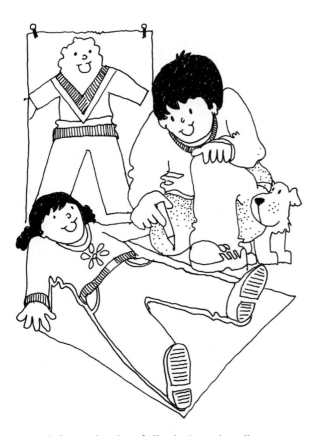

Bright and colourfully designed wall paper can be used to make the cut out look more interesting. Alternatively your child could draw a picture of herself on the plain side and colour or paint the picture to look like the clothes that she is wearing.

Hands and feet

Ask your child to spread her hand out on a sheet of paper and then to draw round it, being especially careful to draw in and out around each finger. She can then cut out and colour the outline shape of her hand.

Feet too can be recorded in this interesting way. Ask her to find out if the outline of her foot fits comfortably inside an outline drawn around her favourite pair of shoes.

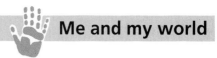

Fingerprints, hand prints and footprints

This is very messy and great fun. You will need some ready mixed paint (although an ink pad for rubber stamps would be perfect for fingerprints if you can get one), sheets of plain paper large enough for the hand prints and perhaps the back of a strip of wallpaper (not the pre-pasted kind) for foot prints.

Let your child use a sponge to dab paint onto the soles of her feet and then walk along the wallpaper strip placed on a hard floor. The number of footprints will depend on the type of paint used and the amount dabbed on.

Hand prints and fingerprints are easier. The secret for a good print is not to use too much paint. When you are both expert at taking prints collect prints from all the family and compare them. Look for whirls, loops and arches, no two prints are the same.

Track records

Occasionally you may come across animal tracks in soft ground. This is one way to make a permanent record of an interesting set of prints.

You will need to get a bag of Plaster of Paris from a chemist or fine builder's plaster from a builder's merchant or DIY shop, an old mixing bowl and wooden spoon and stiff card or strips of wood about 1 inch (2 to 3 cms.) wide.

If there is a soft muddy patch near home, or an area of soft, fine sand (which you can buy in small bags quite cheaply), you can lead a pet dog or cat across it and obtain a good set of prints. Alternatively, your child can make prints of her own hands or feet, or the family car might be used to give an interesting set of tyre tracks.

Whatever you choose, the technique remains the same. Surround the track to be moulded with thick card or wooden strips to form a square or rectangular frame. The frame can be held in position with modelling clay or tape. Get your child to add small amounts of water to the plaster powder in a bowl, stirring steadily and continuously until it takes on the consistency of thick cream.

If the distance is quite long your child could use pencils laid end to end or count the number of hand spans, that is with fingers spread and measuring from the tip of the thumb to the tip of the little finger, that she needs to equal the distance.

Ask her to pour the mixture into the frame around the print. Plaster of Paris sets very quickly, but if possible leave the cast for about half an hour to set hard. Then carefully lift the frame and plaster cast clear of the ground. If all has gone well you will have an exact copy of the print on a plaster base which, once it has dried out, can be painted to set off the three dimensional quality of the cast.

Measuring in spans and paces

Whenever an activity needs some form of measurement of length or distance by your child it isn't necessary for her to use a ruler. In fact, for young children, it is far better that they use what are called "arbitrary or non-standard units". This might be the number of play bricks that she must line up to equal the distance, or the number of marbles, conkers, pebbles or even one pence pieces that are approximately equal to the distance to be measured.

For longer distances still it might require the number of foot lengths, heel to toe, or even paces. For example she can measure in paces how far she can throw a ball which is also a very good way to develop her counting skills.

All kinds of body measurements were used long before rulers. The Egyptians used the cubit which is the distance from finger tips to the elbow and the sailor's fathom was the distance between the outstretched hands of a tall man. Some are still referred to today, like feet and hands. Horses are still measured in "hands" which was the distance across the palm of a large hand, although today it is set at 4 inches (about 10 cms).

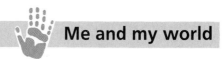

THE FIVE SENSES

Some of the most important parts of our body are designed to allow us to explore the world around us. They give us pictures of our surroundings; visual pictures through our eyes, sound pictures through our ears and a sensual awareness through touch. Our senses of smell and taste help to enhance this awareness.

Although we rely on our senses so much, they are often taken for granted, so it is very interesting to focus on just one at a time to discover how useful they each can be.

Our eyes

Eyes are quite fascinating. Let your child carefully examine her own in a mirror. Are yours the same colour as hers? Point out to her the very fine hairs, the eyelashes, above and below the eye. Blink several times deliberately and slowly to watch how the eyelid sweeps over the eye to wash clean the transparent covering over the front of the eye, the cornea. Look at the coloured part, the iris, very closely to see how it is made. It is like the iris of a camera lens opening or closing the hole at the centre, the pupil.

Spend a few minutes together in a room with dim lighting. Make sure that you have a mirror and a torch available. Wait until your eyes have become accustomed to the low light level, then ask your child to look in the mirror and see the size of her pupils, the central black hole that lets the light through into the eye.

Get her to look at the size of your pupils as well, then tell her to flash the beam of the torch into one of your eyes. Ask her to watch closely to see what happens.

In low light the pupils open very wide to let in as much light as possible. But when she shines the torch into your eye the pupil immediately closes up to shut out the sudden and unexpected bright light. Let her try it on herself while watching in the mirror.

How well can I see?

At the doctor's or the health clinic eye tests are done using special charts, but you can do your own eye testing using a simple home made picture chart.

Cut out of an old magazine or comic some simple, bold shapes like a tree, a house, a flower, a bus, a dog etc. Make sure that some are large

Me and my world

with one or two being quite small. Paste them onto a large sheet of paper or card with the largest shape at the top and getting smaller as you move down the sheet. (In much the same way as a traditional eye test chart).

Place your chart at the far end of a room and ask your child to look at the pictures and tell you what they are. Start by covering the left eye and looking with her right. Note down the number that she gets right, then repeat the test with her left eye to see if there is any difference in ability.

What colour is easiest to see?

This simple test can be repeated in a similar way using bold shapes like squares, circles or triangles coloured differently.

For example draw six squares of the same size on a piece of card or paper. Colour each one differently with paint or felt-tipped pen. Use red, yellow, green, brown, blue and black on a white background.

Place your chart at one end of the garden and lead your child towards it asking her to tell you which coloured shape she sees first? Note down the order in which the various coloured shapes become clearly visible.

You can repeat this test a number of times trying different colour combinations like a red triangle on a yellow background or a purple circle on a blue background. Which combinations of colours does your child see most clearly? What colours does she think warning signs should be so that they are clearly visible?

When you are both out walking or riding in a car or bus look out for road signs. What combinations of colour do the sign makers use, are they easy to see? Don't forget that at night some colours look very strange in the yellow street lights, a good colour in daylight may be very difficult to see at night.

Moving in the dark

Most of us rely so much on our sight that it can be a little frightening but very educational to discover what it is like when we can no longer see.

Take your child to one end of a familiar room. Ask her to have a good look around. Tell her to take note of where chairs, tables and other pieces of furniture might be.

12

Now blindfold her and ask her to go to certain parts of the room or retrieve things placed around the room. You might say, "Go to the television," or, "Get the newspaper that's on top of the table". Always be on hand to stop serious injury, but watch as her confidence builds and her memory-map of the room develops.

When the minute is up cover them over again and see how many she can remember.

Kim's game

Arrange 10 things (like a pair of scissors, a pencil, an egg cup, a clothes peg, a fork etc.) on a tray or table top and cover them with a cloth.

Tell your child that you are going to remove the cloth and that she will have one minute to look at the objects underneath.

There are lots of variations on this simple game, try these:

What's missing?

Set the game up as before, but this time let her turn to look at the objects and when one minute has passed she should turn away again while you remove one of the things on the tray.

Ask her to turn back and look carefully at the things left on the tray to see if she can work out what is missing.

This can be done over and over again.

Using the sense of touch

What can you feel?

You will need a scarf to be used as a blindfold and a number of familiar objects like a pair of scissors, a spoon, a favourite small toy, an apple, a pencil and perhaps some less familiar things like an earring, a bottle top, a coin, a button and a stone.

Blindfold your child and put the familiar things one at a time into her hands. Ask her what they are, and to describe to you what they feel like (cold, hard, heavy, soft, warm and so on).

The other items may be less familiar when relying upon touch alone but, once again, encourage her to describe how they feel and to guess what they might be. (An hilarious party game can be organised in much the same way by passing things hidden under a sheet or table cloth so that the children can only feel them. Cold sausages and plastic bags full of jelly, pickled onions and plastic spiders take on a whole new identity when they cannot be seen).

An interesting alternative to the blindfold test is to put together a group of simple things like keys, a bottle, a small toy and a rubber. Give her a few moments to feel each object then remove one and ask her to feel the things again to try to work out which one is missing.

Playing footsie

Use the blindfold again, but this time ask your child to take her shoes and socks off first. Now lead her over different surfaces and ask her to guess what she is walking on and to tell you what it feels like. Try a stony, gritty concrete path; a spikey, grassy area; cold, hard lino; a bristly door mat or a soft, furry rug; crunchy,

crackly Autumn leaves and soggy, wet newspapers. Encourage her to use as many new words as possible to describe the surfaces.

Our sense of taste

What does it taste like?

Get five or six pots each containing a different food or flavouring. Using a spoon, put a little of the first into your child's mouth. (It is better if she cannot see it – so out with the blindfold again or trust her to keep her eyes closed.) See if she can guess what it is and ask her to describe what it is like; mushy, crunchy, smooth or lumpy, sweet or sour, salty or acidic and vinegary.

Take a little of each in turn using a clean spoon each time so as not to confuse the tastes. It may also be a wise precaution to have a bowl

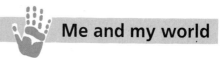

nearby in case something tastes too nasty to swallow, and a sip of water between each will help to clear her palette.

or fruit gums, which includes her favourite, and pop them one at a time into her mouth (but with her eyes shut tight so that she can't see the colours). Does she really know when she has eaten the one that she says she likes best?

Try groups of similar things such as pieces of fruit, cooked or uncooked vegetables, and perhaps a number of different liquids like tea, coffee, cooking oil, vinegar, fruit juice and milk.

Favourite flavours

Children often say that they have a favourite fruit gum or coloured chocolate drop, but is it the colour or the flavour that affects their choice?

Get your child's favourite pack of coloured sweets and ask her what her particular favourite might be. Challenge her to identify it from the others by taste alone. Take three chocolate drops

Taste and smell

It is our sense of smell that prepares our taste buds for the treat that is coming just before we bite into our favourite foods. Both taste and smell mingle to give us a complete flavour picture.

Try this challenge with your child. Get different flavours of potato crisps including her favourite but, before popping in each crisp, pinch her nose and keep it pinched while she munches so that she cannot use her sense of smell to help identify the taste. Can she still pick out her favourite flavour?

Our sense of smell

What does it smell like?

This test can be done in very much the same way as the taste test. Once again it is better if your child cannot see the things, so on with the blindfold once more. Now pass each item under her nose and ask her to tell you what she thinks it might be.

Anything smelly will do. Obvious choices would include fruits like banana, lemon, orange and melon and the just cooked smells from foods such as sausages, boiled eggs, hot buttered toast, fish and onions.

It is also worth trying the more subtle smells of things like the delicate perfume of a flower, fresh bread, a leather bag and the aroma of coffee beans.

Using our ears

What does it sound like?

Collect five or six jars or tins that you can't see into once the lid is screwed on. You will also need a few simple things like a small pile of coins, some marbles, some sand, teaspoons, buttons and pins.

Put the different things into the tins and screw on the lid. Then ask your child to shake each tin in turn and try to discover, from the sounds that they make, what might be hiding inside.

With practice, children can become very good at this game but you can occasionally try to catch them out by putting something like cotton wool in one of the tins, although you will invariably be accused of cheating!

Chinese whispers

Although traditionally played as a game, this is a perfect way to develop children's listening skills.

It is best played by teams of children and can be an outdoor as well as an indoor game.

Give the first child a simple message such as, "We will have a glass of milk and some jam sandwiches in ten minutes time". She must then go to the next child in line (arrange things so that there is a reasonable gap between the children so that one cannot overhear the message being passed to another).

Each child in turn whispers the message to the next in line until it reaches the last child who must come back to you and say out loud what they were told.

It is amazing how distorted and confused a simple message can become by the time it gets back to you.

Can you hear a pin drop?

Just how acute is our hearing? How quiet must a sound be before we are no longer aware of it? This is an opportunity for all the family to take part in a simple test.

You will need something that will make a quiet sound and enough space to do the test in. For example a dried pea, or a pin, or a small button dropped into a plastic box or a tin lid from the same height each time could provide the sound and a long hallway or outside in the garden should be a sufficient distance.

All those taking part should line up facing away from the tester who warns them that the sound is coming and that they should put up a hand as soon as they hear it.

Start with the group close to the tester and, everytime they hear the sound, they should walk forward a couple of paces. This should be repeated until the last person left in the game can no longer hear the sound.

Who has the sharpest sense of hearing?

Where is it coming from?

Some animals have very large ears that they can turn and direct towards strange sounds. Their sense of sound direction is extremely good and helps to keep them alive by picking up danger signals in the wild. But even humans can tell the direction of a sound quite accurately.

Once again a blindfold will be useful. Cover your child's eyes in a quiet room and move away from her and to one side. Make a gently continuous sound, perhaps whistle quietly or hum or clap your hands softly.

Explain to your child that she should turn to face where she thinks the sound is coming from and point at the sound. Let her peep to see how well she did, then try again from a different spot.

THE LIVING WORLD

No child can fail to show at least a passing interest in some of the tens of thousands of different kinds of plants and animals that they will see around them.

Our children will inherit a world that is already facing major ecological problems created by over-intensive farming, over fishing, massive land clearance and deforestation as well as problems due to industrial pollution such as acid rain and destruction of our protective ozone layer.

Never before has there been such a need for every individual to be aware of their responsibility in protecting our natural habitat and every child's interest and curiosity should, at some time, be directed towards an appreciation of the need to nurture and care for that habitat.

This can be achieved in the simplest of ways. When your child shows an interest in some living thing, encourage her to look at it closely and to come to understand something of its life by watching it in its own little world without disturbing it too much. It is such a temptation to pick a beautiful flower or capture an interesting looking insect only to watch it die a short time afterwards.

Spotting and identifying

One activity that will teach your child a great deal about the natural world is to go ''spotting.''

Fortunately we are not just restricted to commercial enterprises like zoos, wildlife parks or working farms, but we also have so many different natural habitats to choose from: forests, moorland, rivers and streams, rock pools and sandy beaches, mountains and marshes, the list seems endless.

Look out for books and other publications

that will help you to identify the main things that you will find. Guides that are full of photographs or accurate, full-colour illustrations and informative text may seem expensive but they will prove to be invaluable and will add an extra dimension to any walk in the country for years to come. The ability to observe closely and to identify and classify are essential skills for any scientist.

Making things grow

This investigation will help your child to understand some of the factors that help plants to grow well.

All that is needed is a pack of seeds, some yogurt pots, margarine tubs or other suitable containers, a small pack of potting medium or sifted soil and some cotton wool.

Suitable seeds would include mustard and cress, runner beans, sweet corn or anything that has a quick germination time and rapid initial growth.

Ask your child what she thinks plants need to make them grow well. Do they need soil, or can they grow without? Do they need water? What happens to plants kept in the dark, will they grow? Should they be kept cool or placed where it is warm? Encourage her to consider these options and to guess what might be better for the plants.

Now let's find out.

Help your child to divide the seeds into eight roughly equal groups. Put one into a pot with dry cotton wool at the bottom and another group into a similar pot with cotton wool, but this time let her water the seeds with sufficient water to thoroughly dampen the cotton wool.

Ask your child to put a third group of seeds into an empty pot and the fourth into a pot half full of potting compost or sifted soil. Help her to cover the seeds with a sprinkling of soil and ask her to add a similar amount of water to BOTH pots, so that the soil is well watered.

The remaining groups of seeds should be put into similar pots, each containing potting compost and covered with a sprinkling of soil as before. Let your child water each of these with equal amounts of water and ask her to place one in a very warm spot (on the window sill in summer or over a radiator in winter) and another where it is quite cold (perhaps a cold garage or even in the fridge!). The remaining two pots should be placed near to one another in a sunny position, but ask your child to make a cover for one out of a cardboard box or dark paper so that the sunlight cannot reach it.

It is important to establish a routine at about the same time each day to check each pot and get your child to add the same amount of water to each pot, except for the one that is being kept dry. One or two of the pots, especially where growth is not occurring, will quickly become water logged unless a few holes have been made in the bottom of the pots to allow the excess to drain away. However, leave the seeds in the empty pot swimming in water as this will help to show the effects of too much water which can be as damaging as too little.

Within a very short time differences in growth will become evident. The seeds with no water will not germinate and will not even begin to grow, whereas those on damp cotton wool will be growing quite well.

Seeds left in water alone will begin to grow, but too much water and no base to grow on (like the cotton wool or the soil) will eventually kill the seedlings. Those growing in the soil will probably be quite healthy.

The seeds kept in the warm will probably begin to grow faster than those kept cold, especially if they have been left in the fridge where the seeds would be deprived of warmth and light.

Interestingly, plants grown under a cover do grow, and can be quite tall. But when compared with normal plants they appear yellow and spindly and if they continued to grow in the dark they would eventually die.

Although you can never guarantee what will happen to seedlings your child will inevitably learn a lot about plant care and the conditions necessary for good growth. She could perhaps employ her new found skills by growing flowers and vegetables in a small plot in the garden.

Water

Free play

The importance of play in education should never be underestimated. Children should be given every opportunity for free play because so much can be discovered through their own undirected exploration.

An activity that lends itself to learning in this way uses one of the commonest substances, yet one that is vital to life: water.

Bath time is an obvious occasion for water play, but, if possible, obtain a large bowl or trough for the garden, or even a blow up plastic paddling pool.

Collect as many different bottles and containers as you can (plastic rather than glass) so that your child can fill and pour, squirt and sprinkle the water.

It is helpful if some of the jugs, bottles and jars are transparent so that the level of water in them can be clearly seen. We will be using these for a number of investigations at a later stage.

Filling and pouring

How well can your child pour? Can she empty one container into another without losing any of the water? Even as adults it is not always as easy as it seems, although I tend to blame the teapot rather than myself!

Some narrow necked bottles can be hard to pour into. A funnel shape cut from the top of a washing up liquid bottle can help.

Push the point of some scissors into the side of the bottle about 4 inches (10 cms.) below the neck and cut carefully round.

Sizing them up

Collect a number of different containers and ask your child to put them in order, from the one that she thinks will hold the most water down to the one that will hold the least. Using a small jug or cup, and using her new funnel to help pour, she can find out how many times it has to be filled and poured to fill each of the containers.

liquid. For example: litre bottles of lemonade, washing detergent and shampoo, and containers for ice cream and margarine.

Check beforehand that they actually hold about the same amount of water then ask your child to guess which one will hold the most. The eye is easily deceived and children often choose the taller containers.

Let her fill each in turn with a litre measuring jug or something similar, or pour water from one into another to discover that they actually hold the same amount.

Was her order correct? Often some tall, slender bottles look as though they should hold a great deal but actually take less than some shorter, squatter containers.

Deceiving the eye

Collect a number of different shaped containers that are all designed to hold the same amount of

It can be quite a surprise to find that they are all the same, especially when the container that was thought to be the largest is filled with water and poured into the "smallest" only to discover that, far from overflowing, it actually takes every drop.

Squirter power

This outdoor activity can be great fun. Prise off the top of a washing up liquid bottle and fill the bottle full of water. Replace the top and squeeze.

Ask your child how she might make the water jet go the greatest distance. Let her feel the force of the water jet. Let her feel it when you squeeze gently and when you are squeezing as hard as possible.

The harder she squeezes the further it goes but does the size of the hole matter? Let her try squirting the bottle with the top removed, this is a much larger hole but does the water go so far? To squirt the greatest distance should the bottle be held level with the ground or up at an angle? Is there more force when the bottle is full or half empty?

Organise competitions to see who can squirt the furthest and also with the greatest accuracy. Place a target, perhaps a bucket or paddling pool, a good distance away and see who can hit the target every time. Alternatively, empty drink cans can be piled in pyramid fashion to see who can knock the whole pile down.

Where is the water level?

Take a variety of transparent containers, the more unusual the shape the better, half fill with water and replace the lid. Get your child to notice the postion of the water's surface when the containers are placed on a table top. Ask what will happen when they are slowly tilted, will the water level tilt too? Let her investigate by tilting the bottles in every possible direction. (In all cases the water level remains constantly horizontal to the ground.)

As a further test to check her understanding, draw a drinking glass in the positions shown in the diagram and ask your child to show where the water level would be if it was half full of water. Let her check her drawings with a real glass.

Pipes and funnels

Clear plastic tubing can be bought from many places especially where home-made wine and beer kits are sold. They often have plastic funnels too. It is great fun to fix a funnel in each end of a length of tube and watch how the water pours from one end out of the other.

Get your child to coil the tube into a confusion of twists and turns, then while you hold one end she can pour water from a large jug into the other end. So long as the end being filled is at the highest point the water will always drain through. (A little ink or food colouring added to the water makes it easier to watch as it flows through the coils.)

While you hold the funnels exactly level get your child to pour in water until both funnels are about half full.

Ask her what will happen to the water levels if one funnel is raised slightly? Let her try for herself. Can she fill one funnel just by moving the other? Which way should the funnel be moved, up or down?

A water syphon

All that you need to make the syphon is a piece of clear plastic tube about one metre long.

Ask your child to fill the tube completely with water and hold the ends closed with her thumbs. This can be done quite easily by holding the tube under the surface of the water in a large bowl until all the air has bubbled out.

If one end is left in the water and the other end is held lower than the bowl, the water will appear to flow up the tube and then out through the lower end. Air pressure on the surface of the water in the bowl is forcing the water through the tube and down to a lower level, but this will only happen if the tube is COMPLETELY full of water, any air pockets left in the tube will stop the flow.

This syphoning technique is often used to empty fish tanks. Ask your child to find out what happens to the speed of flow when the lower end is slowly raised? At what point does the water flow stop?

Air pockets

If a plastic tumbler is plunged upside down into a deep bowl or sink the air is trapped inside. This is often rather difficult to see so how can we prove it?

Ask your child to roll some tissue paper into a ball and watch what happens when she puts it into a bowl of water. It very quickly becomes saturated and you are in no doubt that it is soaked right through.

Now ask her to roll a second tissue ball and wedge it firmly into the bottom of a dry glass so that it won't fall out when turned upside down.

Holding the glass upside down get her to push the glass carefully but firmly under the surface of the water in a deep bowl or the bath.

Has the glass filled with water? Ask her to remove the glass and take out the ball of tissue. Is it soaking wet? You will probably find that, apart from a few stray drops of water, the tissue is quite dry because the air trapped in the glass stopped the water from flooding in. People have been known to survive for hours and even days breathing air caught in air pockets inside a sunken boat.

Pouring air

In exactly the same way as the previous experiment, ask your child to push an empty glass upside down into a bowl or bath of water.

By carefully tilting the tumbler the air can be poured out under the surface of the water and it can be seen bubbling to the top.

Get another glass and push this under in the same way, holding it below the other glass that is now full of water. The air can now be poured from one to the other. As the bubbles of air rise into the full tumbler the water is forced out. With care and a little practice your child will find that she can pour the air back and forth.

Test your lungs

If a large bottle is placed in a deep bowl so that it fills with water the bottle can be turned upside down and lifted out of the water. As long as the mouth of the bottle stays below the water's surface in the bowl, air pressure on the surface will keep the water inside the bottle.

Let your child put one end of a length of plastic tubing up into the neck of the bottle and blow gently down the other end. The air will bubble up into the bottle forcing the water out.

Blow football

You will need a large flat surface, like a table top, a table tennis ball, some pipe cleaners and some large straws (the wide ones popular in fast food restaurants are perfect).

First of all help your child to make two goals. Each goal is made from three straws and pieces of pipe cleaner. Cut two of the straws at about one third of their length to make the two uprights and two supporting pieces. The third straw is the cross bar. Cut pieces of pipe cleaner about 2 inches (5 cms.) long. Twist them together to make joints for the pieces of straw.

You could test the size of your lungs in this way. Fill lots of bottles with water and while one person holds each one in turn see how many can be emptied by blowing down the tube using only one puff.

Stand each goal at either end of the table and use another straw each to blow the ball. (You may wish to put books, play bricks or similar obstacles around the edge of the table to stop the ball from continually falling off).

Floating and sinking

Your child may have noticed that when a container is full of water it sinks but when it is partly or completely full of air it tends to float to the surface. Blowing air into a bottle full of water will make it rise to the surface like a submarine blowing its sea water tanks. Whether or not something will float is determined by what kind of material it is made of (eg. wood, plastic, metal, paper) and its shape, especially how much air the shape can contain.

The first thing to be done is to collect a large number of things of all shapes and sizes and made from a wide range of materials. Collect rubbers, plasticene, pen tops, screws, pencil stubs, pieces of wood, pegs, tin lids, stones, cork, pieces of pottery, nuts and bolts, buttons, plastic bricks, milk bottle tops and so on. The more different items you can find the better.

Help your child to sort the objects by what they are made from. Make collections of wooden things, metal things and things made from plastic, things made from rubber and glass and clay, stone and paper etc.

Ask your child to decide which might float and which will sink. Let her feel the objects, how heavy or light they might be. When she has made her guesses let her try each one in turn to see. Encourage her to place them carefully into the water.

Make sets of the things that will float and the things that won't. As she continues to test things can she predict more accurately what will and what will not float?

Plasticene boats

Sometimes a heavy object will float if it covers a wide area and contains air, like a saucer or a tin lid, but if it is upset and water spills in, it will sink.

Offer a ball of modelling clay the size of a small apple to your child and ask if she can make it float. If she simply puts hers into some water it will sink every time, so after a couple of failures suggest that it might help if the shape is changed. She will see that the flatter the shape the longer it takes to sink until she realises that if the sides are curled up to make a broad, saucer shape the plasticene will float very well.

To be successful it is necessary for the plasticene to be squashed quite thin, a rolling pin introduced at the right time would be very helpful.

Boat testing

If she has been successful in making modelling clay boats let her test them by discovering which one will hold the greatest weight before sinking.

You will need to provide things like wood or plastic play bricks, marbles, small stones or even conkers which can be used as weights.

Get her to load her boat carefully with the weights, counting how many it will carry before the water laps over the sides and it sinks. If possible let her compare two or three different boat shapes, including perhaps one that you have made.

Discover the most successful boat shape and discuss how its shape might have made it so efficient.

Where do floaters float?

Ask your child to take a number of the things from her set of floaters in the floating and sinking test. Get her to put them carefully into a large bowl of water. If you have a clear sided tank, like a small fish tank, this is even better.

How well do they float? How much of each thing is above the water's surface and how much is below? Polystyrene is often used as a packing material for large items. If you can get a good sized piece see where it floats (much of it will be above the water) let your child try to push it under the water, it is very hard to do. Polystyrene would make a good swimming float.

How much of a piece of wood is above the surface and how much is below? Let your child try with different kinds of wood of a similar size. Does cork float higher in the water than softwood, does a hardwood like oak float higher or lower than pine?

Ask her if she thinks fresh fruit will float. Try a tomato or an apple, does the variety of apple change the height at which it floats? Ask her to guess which way up a pear will float, point up or down?

Add a large amount of salt to the water and ask if this will have any effect? Try putting the floaters into fresh water and then into the strongly salted water. Get your child to look very carefully, is there any difference in the height at which they float? (The salted water is denser than pure water and so things float more easily in it, as in the Dead Sea in Jordan.) Perhaps this investigation will help her to understand why it is often easier to swim in sea water than in fresh.

What disappears in water?

When you add salt to water it seems to disappear. Get your child to add a spoonful to a tumbler of water and stir. The salt dissolves and can no longer be seen but if she tastes the water she will know that it is still there.

What other things dissolve in water?

Help your child to find household substances that she can try to dissolve in water. Choose things like sugar, coffee granules, flour, tea leaves, soap powder, gravy powder or granules, crushed cornflakes, and any other HARMLESS powdered foods or additives that you may have to hand.

Some things disappear very quickly but others may need a little help. Suggest stirring or shaking as this often helps. Make a set of the things that dissolve easily (salt, sugar etc.).

Get your child to try the others again, but this time using hot (NOT BOILING) water. Stir well and look carefully. Tea-leaves colour the water so something has dissolved but the leaves are left behind. (Try red cabbage too, which turns the water blue.) Gravy powder or granules dissolve but make the water thick and brown, they seem to change the water in some way.

Collect together the things that only partly dissolve and note the kinds of things that don't dissolve at all.

Also get her to notice that when lots of sugar is put into cold water only some of the sugar dissolves, but when you use hot water far more sugar dissolves and it "disappears" much more quickly.

Puddle watching

If you have been left with a large puddle after heavy rain try this investigation which will help your child to understand what evaporation means.

It is important that the puddle should be in a dip in a concrete or tarmaced surface, not on a grass or packed earth surface which will allow the water to soak away rather than evaporate.

Using ordinary blackboard chalk ask your child to draw round the edge of the puddle. Leave the puddle for 15 to 20 minutes then come back and ask her to draw round it again. Keep doing this until the whole puddle has disappeared.

The chalk lines are a good visual record of the speed with which the water evaporated from the puddle. An older child may find it interesting to discover just how much water has gone by refilling the dip to each of the chalk lines. There is no need to use a measuring jug, she can measure in cupfuls or bottlefuls.

Try to find how many cupfuls of water have evaporated from the whole puddle and how long it took.

Blowing bubbles

Blowing bubbles is always great fun, but can you blow giant bubbles or double-bubbles? All that you will need is some washing up liquid, a bowl for your bubble mixture, some wire that can be bent easily into different shapes (florists wire or thick fuse wire for example) and a funnel (the top cut from an empty washing up liquid bottle would be perfect).

If you dissolve soap flakes in water and blow air through the mixture using drinking straws, hundreds of tiny bubbles will froth up, but this mixture will not make good sized bubbles.

For bubble blowing try a strong solution of washing up liquid, (half liquid and half water). Let your child make a variety of rings from florists wire or thicker fuse wire.

There is no one right way to blow good bubbles. Some people favour a strong steady blow while others pull the loop quickly through the air and let the bubbles stream out the back.

Ask your child to find out if the size of the loop alters the size of the bubble. Does a square ring make a square bubble? What happens when she blows through a double or treble loop, does she get double bubbles?

Let her try dipping the wide end of a funnel into the bubble mixture and then blow down the narrow stem. This can take quite a bit of puff but with care she will get giant bubbles.

Find as many things as you can with a hole in to see if she can get bubbles from them, even a small sieve perhaps!

(One word of warning, when your child is tired of bubble blowing make sure she rinses her hands and mouth well to remove the concentrated soap solution.)

Making waves

Ripples in a pond move outwards in regular ring patterns but can your child guess what shape the ripples will make if, for instance, a square brick is dropped into a large puddle?

Let your child try different shapes and sizes. Ask her if a large brick will make larger ripples.

Are the ripples closer together or further apart if an object is dropped from a greater height, and what happens if two things are dropped in at the same time, are there double ripples?

Get your child to tap the surface gently and slowly with a stick. Ask her to tap more quickly, are the ripples closer together or further apart?

Keeping dry

What should we wear when it is raining? What sort of material is best at keeping the water out?

You will need pieces of material about 1 foot (30 cms.) square. Include net curtaining, knitted wool, PVC cloth, heavy coat material, plastic sheeting and waxed cotton if possible, as well as other more usual fabrics. (Pieces cut from old clothes or shop bought remnants would be fine.)

Ask your child to sort them out into piles, those that she thinks will keep her dry and the others that would let water through.

Show her how to wrap the material squares over the top of glass or plastic tumblers that are half full of water. Secure each one in position with an elastic band.

Now get her to turn each covered tumbler upside down, one at a time. Ask her to watch carefully to see if any of the water seeps through. With some of the materials the water will drip out quite quickly, others may resist for a while but, when the water has thoroughly soaked the material, some will begin to drip through.

Are there any material samples that stop all water from coming through? Would they make good fabrics for macs or anoraks? (Plastic sheeting might stop water from coming through but ask your child if she would really want to wear clothes made from it?)

Drying out

How long do different materials take to dry out?

Use the squares of material from the previous investigation. Ask your child to place them in a large bowl or sink and cover them with water. Let the pieces soak through then take each in turn and help her to hang them on the washing line to dry.

Ask her to guess which will dry first and which will be the last to dry. Go together to check periodically by feeling each piece of material to see if it is drying. You must agree between you when a piece feels dry or when it may still feel damp.

How accurate was her guess work? Discover which materials dry first. How much longer do the other materials take and which material takes the longest? (A piece of heavy fur fabric can take a very long time indeed).

Best drying conditions

Ask your child where she thinks clothes will dry fastest? Take a number of handkerchiefs or pieces of cloth that are the same size and made from the same material and soak them well for the same length of time.

Ask your child to place each one in a different spot, some indoors and some outside. Does a handkerchief hung on a radiator dry faster than another blowing in a brisk wind on a clothes line? Will one hung on a clothes airer indoors dry faster than another in a still, shaded corner outside?

When all the pieces have been placed ask her to guess which will dry quickly and which will take the longest time. Once again, check together by feeling each one to decide when they are dry. Warmth and a brisk breeze can aid the rapid evaporation of water. It is possible that material outside in a strong wind can dry faster than a piece left on a radiator.

Watching the weather

Air contains water in the form of vapour that has evaporated not only from puddles and people's washing, but from lakes, rivers and the sea. The vapour forms clouds; high, wispy patches of ice particles (called cirrus), thick blankets (called stratus) and thundery clouds like heavy mounds of cotton wool (cumulus). We notice it most of course when it falls back to the ground as rain, sleet, snow or hail or early in the morning as dew.

One way of studying the weather is to keep a simple day by day record:

Measuring rainfall

Rainfall is measured in inches or centimetres by collecting it in a suitable container.

Help your child to cut the top quarter off an empty washing up liquid bottle by pushing the point of a pair of scissors through the plastic and then cutting round. Pull off the squirter top and push it upside down into the base of the bottle so that it acts like a funnel.

The rain trap should be left out in the open, but where it will not be accidently knocked over. Get your child to check each day to see what has been collected. She should take out the funnel and put a stick into the bottle to touch the bottom, like using a dip stick on a car to check the oil level.

If it has been raining, the stick will be wet and all that she needs to do is measure how much of it is wet with a ruler or tape measure. Alternatively, the stick can be marked at 1cm. intervals. Get her to measure to the nearest centimetre mark, then empty the container and replace the stick ready for another day.

Wind direction

A very simple wind vane can be made using a piece of card cut from an empty cereal packet, a drinking straw, a wire coat hanger, a wood or plastic bead or a large button and a piece of wood about 1 foot (30cms.) square as the base.

Help your child to draw and cut out a large arrow shape as shown, about 1 foot (30cms.) long, from the card. Sellotape the straw to the side of it about 1 inch (2 to 3cms.) in front of the half way point along the arrow's length.

Using a strong pair of pliers, snip off the twisted part of the hanger and bend it as shown. The triangular bends at the bottom will make it easy to stand it on the wooden base.

A bead or large button threaded over the wire to rest on the kink in the wire will support the straw on the wind vane and allow it to turn freely.

It is important to set up the vane in the same way each time. Paint or write the compass points north, south, east and west onto the base and, using a compass or some other means of determining north, point the north marked on the base in the right direction.

Remember to explain that the direction that the vane points in is the direction that the wind is coming FROM. A north wind is very cold because it is coming from the frozen north, a southerly wind is coming from the warmer, tropical zones.

If you are unable to make a vane, but the approximate directions of north, south-east and west are known, suggest that your child holds up a handkerchief in the breeze or throws a handful of grass cuttings into the air which will give an indication of the wind's direction.

Keeping weather records

| NO WIND | LIGHT WIND | FRESH/BRISK WIND | GALE | HURRICANE |

These are best done on a piece of plain paper marked at the top with the days of the week. Encourage your child to make her observations at about the same time each day, perhaps mid morning.

Set out the chart as shown so that it is easy to fill in the following information:

1 The number of marks covered (or centimetres measured) on the rainfall dip-stick.
2 The wind direction, north, south, east or west, taken to the nearest compass point.
3 A picture to show the speed of the wind similar to the examples shown.
4 A picture to show how much sun or cloud she can see.

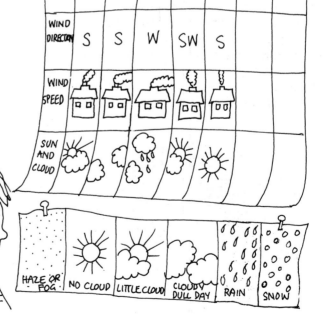

Energy

HOT AND COLD

How do we keep some things hot and stop other things from melting? Some corner shops wrap blocks of ice cream in layers of newspaper. Does it really help to stop the ice cream from getting soft before you get home? And why do we put a cosy over the tea pot?

Keeping warm

Lay out some of your child's clothes. Have things like a cotton T-shirt, shorts, an anorak, a woolly jumper, a scarf, swim wear, night clothes, a coat and so on.

You will also need two jars. It isn't often that we have two identical teapots but any two similar containers with lids will do.

Ask her what she would wear to stay cool on a hot, summer's day and what she would wear to keep warm on a cold winter's day.

Half fill both of the jars with water that feels hot. (Do NOT use very hot or boiling water.) Screw on the lids.

Ask your child what she would do to keep one of the jars as warm as possible. Let her think about the kinds of clothes that would keep her warm and let her wrap her jar in scarves and jumpers. Make sure that the top and bottom are as well covered as the sides. Leave the unwrapped jar by the side of the wrapped one until the unwrapped jar feels quite cold. (This could take anything up to half an hour.)

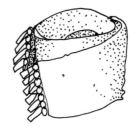 

Unscrew the lid of the jar and let your child feel the water, which will be much colder than at the start. Now unwrap the other jar and let her feel the difference.

The warm clothes have helped to keep the heat in and it will feel much hotter than the water in the jar that was left unwrapped.

Freezing cold

Take an ice cube from the fridge. Watch together the way that it melts. How long does it take? What is the ice turning into? Let your child feel the slippery ice and watch the drips of water forming. It can be too cold to hold for long. If you collect all the water it doesn't look enough to make back into the cube again, why is that? Let's find out.

Caps off

You are going to need a strong plastic bottle, like a lemonade bottle, and space in a freezer.

Ask your child to fill the bottle to the very top so that you can't squeeze another drop in. Make a little cap out of tin foil and cover the top then stand the bottle upright in a freezer and leave it overnight.

As the water freezes it expands and takes up more space. Because the sides of the bottle are strong the only place the ice water can go is out of the top. If you are lucky you will find that the water has frozen and turned into a column of ice sticking up from the neck of the bottle with the little foil cap sitting on the top.

This can happen to milk left on the doorstep on a cold winter's day and water pipes are burst by the water freezing and expanding inside them.

Staying cool

This time you will need lots of ice cubes, two saucers, warm clothes again; scarves, woolly hats and jumpers, and two jars with screw lids.

Melting moments

Give your child two large ice cubes on saucers. Ask her to put one of them somewhere in the house where it will keep cool and stay frozen longer and to put the other where she thinks it might melt quickly. (Back in the fridge is an obvious answer for the first one, but ask her to think of another spot if she chooses it.)

Get her to check the ice cubes from time to time to see which one turns to water first.

What you are doing is showing that, for ice to melt, it needs heat. A warmer place will melt ice faster.

Keeping the cold in

Now help her to fill the two containers with ice cubes. Cram in as many as you can.

Tell her that you want to make one of the jars as warm as possible. Ask her to wrap one of them in the warm clothing as tightly as she can, and don't forget the top and bottom as well as the sides.

Choose a suitable spot like a window ledge or table top and leave both jars side by side.

Ask your child to check the jar that has been left unwrapped to see if the cubes are melting. But tell her NOT to disturb the other jar.

When the cubes are about half melted into a slushy mix of water and ice ask your child what she expects to find when the other jar is unwrapped. Because it has been so snuggly wrapped will it all have been turned into water long ago?

It is always a surprise when the final layer of clothing is pulled away, the ice cubes have hardly begun to melt at all.

When we wear thick, warm clothing it traps our natural body heat inside keeping us warm. But it does an equally good job of trapping the cold of the ice inside and stops the warm air in the room from reaching the jar so that the ice does not have enough warmth to melt by very much. (This also works wonderfully well with snow packed into the jars.)

Warm blooded

If you have a medical thermometer you can show an interesting feature of warm blooded creatures, like us; that is the ability to control our body temperature.

Take your child's temperature and help them to read the scale. Many clinical thermometers have an arrow pointing at normal blood heat (35°C. or 98°F.).

Get her to run around the garden, this can be made even more dramatic if she puts on several layers of warm clothing first. In no time at all she will be feeling extremely hot.

Retake her temperature. You will find that it is still approximately the same, even though she feels much, much hotter.

Sweating is the body's natural way to lose heat. Sweat, which is mainly water and salt, leaks onto the skin's surface and takes some of the body's heat to evaporate away and so cools the skin.

The danger on a very hot day is that we might lose too much water in this way and become dehydrated, so it is important to drink little and often to maintain our body fluid level.

COLOUR AND LIGHT

Some sweets and chocolates come wrapped in coloured cellophane and many products have coloured see-through wrappers. Ask your child to save as many different coloured pieces as she can so that they can be used for a number of interesting experiments on colour and light.

Rose coloured glasses

For this interesting activity you will need scissors, thin card (a strip cut from a cereal packet would be quite suitable), pieces of coloured cellophane, some glue and some sunglasses or ordinary spectacles.

Help your child to draw round the sunglasses onto the strip of thin card. Make sure that she includes the arms of the glasses so that when the shape is cut out the card arms can be bent back to fit over her ears, just like the real thing.

Help her to cut out the holes where the lenses would be fitted and then ask her to choose two pieces of clear cellophane of the same colour.

Ask her to put some glue around the edge of each eye hole and let her stick the pieces of cellophane over the eye holes. Now she can look at the world through coloured glasses.

Ask her to describe the appearance of familiar objects. Let her try different colours; yellow, red, green and blue. Does she feel that a blue world is a better place to live in than perhaps a yellow one?

Help her to find out what happens when she tries to confuse her brain by having red for one eye and green for the other, or yellow for one and blue for the other.

Coloured lights

Torches can be very useful when exploring the effects of coloured light.

If your pieces of coloured cellophane are large enough they can be wrapped around the lens of the torch and held in place with an elastic band.

Help your child to spotlight things in a darkened room, using the coloured beam. Let her discover the change in appearance of a green apple in red light or yellow gloves in blue light.

If you have more than one torch help her to discover the effect of overlapping beams of different colours on a white background. Some very strange combinations can be obtained and she will discover that it is not at all like mixing paints or ink.

Coloured spinners

Another way to mix light is to put areas of colour on circles of card and spin them so that the light seen from each colour mixes together.

You will need some more thin card, coloured felt tipped pens or pencils, some pencil stubs, thin string and scissors.

Help your child to draw and cut out some card circles. Find a jar or a tin about 10cm. (4ins.) across to draw round. Push the stub of a pencil through the centre of the circle and show your child how to spin the circle like a top.

You can experiment using a long pencil instead of the pencil stub. Ask her which one she thinks will spin the longest. She will soon find that the long pencil is more unstable than the short one and quickly topples over.

Let her colour the card circles in different ways; half black, half white, half red, half yellow, with coloured dots or a spiral pattern and so on.

Watch what happens to the patterns when the tops are spun.

Another way to make a spinner is to make two holes either side of the centre of the card circle, thread a metre length of thin twine or wool through the holes and knot the ends.

The string loops are then held around the backs of both hands and by twisting the disc and pulling gently and rhythmically outwards on the strings the card circle can be made to spin so fast that it hums.

Through the looking glass

Mirrors can be a constant source of interest. It is always so difficult to appreciate that the person we see in a mirror is not the person that others see. Putting an earring on our left ear or combing a parting on the left side of our head will appear to be on the right side by someone looking at our reflection in the mirror.

If your child has been learning left and right, ask her to put her hand over her right eye and look in a mirror. Can she work out which eye is being covered by her reflection?

When she waves her left hand which hand does her reflection wave? It can be very confusing.

Distorting mirrors

A fairground hall of mirrors can make us look really silly by distorting our reflections. This is done by bending the mirror slightly in different directions. A similar effect can be seen using shiny table spoons.

Ask your child to look at herself in the bowl of a large spoon. Not only does it make her look odd as she moves the spoon around, but she will also notice that she seems to be upside down.

Ask her to turn the spoon over so that she looks at the back. She will be the right way up, but how strange she looks as the curved surface distorts her reflection.

You may be lucky enough to be able to get a plastic safety mirror. Many mirrors used in schools are silvered plastic sheets which can be gently bent into curved shapes. These show the effects of a curved mirror very clearly and can be great fun. Bending the sides inwards creates a concave shape which, like the bowl of the spoon, can turn images upside down or, when very close up, can magnify your reflection like a shaving mirror. Bending the mirror outwards at the sides to make a convex shape makes your reflection look very wide.

Up periscope

We can use mirrors to bend light round corners. This is a simple way to make something that will let your child look over tall objects, or round the side of a building without being seen.

You will need two mirrors (handbag vanity mirrors will do) and a cardboard tube or box about 2 feet (60 cms.) long and just narrower than the length of each mirror (about 3 to 4 inches or 8 to 10 cms.). A suitable box can be made from a cardboard pack cut to size and held together with sticky tape.

Help your child to cut two slots into the tube or box, one at the top and one at the bottom; at an angle, with two viewing holes as shown.

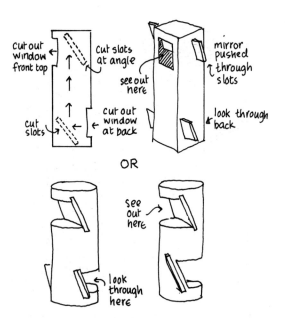

The mirrors can now be pushed into the slots and held securely with more tape.

When your child looks through the lower viewing hole into the bottom mirror she will see whatever is reflected in the top mirror.

Kaleidoscopes

Using the same two handbag mirrors as before ask your child to place them on a table top on their edge and at an angle to one another. Pushing the mirrors into some modelling clay helps them to stand up or their backs can be taped together with Sellotape.

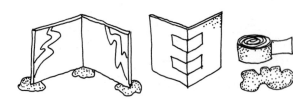

Ask her to put one small object; a small toy, a dice or a colourful stone or bead for example, between the two mirrors. Get her to look in the mirrors, how many reflections can she see? If the mirrors are stood close together at a narrow angle only 2 or 3 reflections will be seen, but as she opens up the angle between the mirrors the number of reflections increases.

Ask her what is the largest number of reflections she can see with only one object.

With the two mirrors set roughly at right angles ask your child to put a group of small colourful things in the angle of the two mirrors (small scraps of brightly coloured paper will do very well). Looking downwards and into the two mirrors she will see a kaleidoscope of colour that will constantly change if she moves the little objects around.

MORE ABOUT SOUND

We hear sound when something vibrates or shakes the air and those vibrations reach our ears. Sound can only travel through something like air, water or even solid objects, but can't travel through empty space.

Earlier investigations explored our sense of hearing, but the following experiments tell us more about sound itself.

Ask your child to put her ear to a table top while you gently tap on the other end. She will be able to hear even your gentlest tapping quite clearly. Try the same thing on a long iron railing or a wall of your home. Sound travels through solid objects more easily than through air.

Help your child to tie some spoons onto a loop of string and then to hold the ends of the strings against each ear. When the spoons are jangled together they sound like chiming bells as

43

help her to direct the funnel towards a watch on a table top or to her own heart beats sounding through her chest.

the sound passes directly up the string and through the bones in the head to the ears.

Megaphones and ear trumpets

Sound can be more easily heard or transmitted further if the sound can be concentrated. The strange shape of our ears is designed to collect as much sound as possible and direct the sound into the ear canal. If we can collect more sound we should be able to hear gentle noises more clearly.

A primitive ear trumpet can be made by rolling a large sheet of paper (a page from a newspaper perhaps) into a cone shape and holding it in place with some sticky tape. Let your child try her ear trumpet to pick up the sound of a ticking clock from across a room and other such quiet sounds.

A simple stethoscope can be made from a length of plastic tube with a funnel in one end. While your child holds the other end to her ear

The ear trumpet design can also be used to make a megaphone. Roll the tube less tightly so that the narrower end is large enough to shout through. A noisy activity, perhaps best kept for a local park or field, but see who can be heard from the greatest distance without the megaphone and how much further the voices travel when shouting through it.

Making music

Children love to play along to tunes and make their own music. Sounds can be made by banging and shaking drums, blocks and containers, blowing into or across the tops of bottles and pipes and plucking, bowing or hitting stretched strings.

Ten green bottles . . .

Collect a number of glass bottles, they can be all shapes and sizes. Ask your child to tap each one gently with the handle of a fork or a small wooden spoon or a pencil and to listen to the sound made. Some will be high notes, some lower, some louder, some softer. Let her try to change the pitch of the note by pouring water into or out of the bottles. Ask her if the note gets higher or lower when more water is added.

Can she "tune" her bottles by adding or removing water and then use them to play a simple medley? Help her to tap out "Three blind mice" or "London's burning." If she has been very successful in tuning her bottles get her to accompany you singing her favourite nursery rhyme?

As an alternative to tapping the bottles help your child to "play" the bottles by blowing across the tops of each one. It is essential to get just the right angle of puff but with practice she will be able to make some very interesting sounds and may eventually be able to play recognisable melodies.

Pan's pipes

If you have an old hose pipe help your child saw the pipe into various lengths. Make one about a foot long (30cms.) and then each successive piece 2 inches (5cms.) shorter.

Using Sellotape or electrical insulating tape join the pieces of pipe together so that the tops of each length are at the same level.

The pipes are played in exactly the same way as the bottles. By blowing across the top of each pipe a series of notes can be sounded. Ask your child if the shorter pipes will make lower or higher pitched sounds.

With this and similar experiments, she will be discovering that shorter pipes or air spaces in bottles produce higher pitched sounds. She will be able to relate this to longer and shorter strings on instruments in later investigations.

Bangers and shakers

Simple rhythm shakers can be made using empty yogurt or margarine pots and some dried peas or beans. You will also need some Sellotape or electrician's insulating tape.

Let your child wash and dry two identical plastic pots then put a handful of dried peas or something similar into one of them. The other pot can then be securely taped to the top of the first. Swirling and shaking the instrument produces some interesting rhythm sounds to accompany favourite songs.

Suitable skins can be made from plastic bags, strong wrapping paper or tightly stretched material. Containers can be chosen from plastic mixing bowls and food storage bowls, or lengths can be cut from the large cardboard tubes used for rolling carpets around, which are often available from carpet shops. In fact any rounded container, with or without a bottom, can be used.

Place your container onto the paper, plastic or material that will act as the drum skin. Ask your child to draw around the container and then make a second circle 3 to 4 inches (8 to 10cms.) larger all round and cut out the larger circle using scissors.

Tom toms and timpani

Drums can be made easily by stretching a "skin" over a hollow container. You will find that the larger the container the deeper the sound produced.

Help her to pull the skin tight over the top of the container and hold it in place with a broad rubber band or length of elastic.

The finished drum can be played with the handles of wooden spoons, pencils or simply by tapping with the fingers.

Elastic band guitar

The previous activity will have shown your child the need for a container as a "sound box" to give volume to the sound. A sound box is essential for most stringed instruments to give the sounds they produce depth and quality. That is why instruments such as guitars, violins and cellos are made principally from a slender neck attached to a curved wooden box with the strings stretched across them.

To gain a little more understanding of these points obtain a cardboard box like an empty tissue box that has a hole cut into its top surface.

Stretch an elastic band between your fingers and ask your child to twange it. The sound will not be very great. Now get her to stretch it over the box and across the hole in the top. When the band is twanged now, the sound is much louder.

This very simple model can be greatly improved if a number of bands are used and if they are stretched across two sticks, either side of the hole, to hold the bands above the surface of the box. Better still if you can find a wooden box to use, a cigar box for example would be perfect.

Your child will soon discover that longer, looser bands give lower notes and bands that are quite short and stretched tight give higher notes when plucked.

Tubular bells

A set of chimes that are very easy to make can produce a delightful sound and, with a little patience, can be tuned to allow recognisable melodies to be played.

Some initial effort is required to obtain some lengths of copper tubing or large nails of various sizes.

Nails can be purchased from a good ironmongers (ask for one each of as many sizes as possible from 3 inches (7.5cms) to 10 inches (25cms.) in length).

Copper tubing can be purchased as off cuts from a plumbers, or as a single length from a D-I-Y store. You will need a hacksaw with a blade for metals to cut the tubes into various lengths.

Try 3 inches (7.5cms) to 12 inches (30cms) in 1 inch steps.

Help your child to tie each tube or nail to a length of cord or string. If necessary they can be held more firmly with pieces of sticky tape. The strings can now be tied onto a cord strung between the uprights of a simple frame made from two pieces of wood nailed to a base.

Your child can play the chimes by tapping them gently with a metal rod, a nail, spoon handle or something similar.

ELECTRICITY

Simple circuits

Electricity is probably one of the most indispensible forms of energy used today. Almost everything we use is either powered by electricity or requires electricity to make it. Yet it is a form of energy that many of us know little about.

The following experiments and investigations will help to give your child an important knowledge and understanding of basic electricity.

IT IS ESSENTIAL THAT YOU MAKE ABSOLUTELY CLEAR THAT, WHILE IT IS PERFECTLY SAFE TO USE THE BATTERIES, WIRES ETC. DESCRIBED ON THESE PAGES, UNDER NO CIRCUMSTANCES SHOULD YOUR CHILD ATTEMPT TO USE THE MAINS ELECTRICAL SUPPLY, WHICH CAN KILL.

Lighting up time

For these simple electrical experiments your child will need a few basic items which you should be able to get from a good electrician or electrical D.I.Y. shop.

Buy two small bulb holders with bulbs (ask for 3.5 volt bulbs which are cheap and easily obtainable, although anything between 3 and 6 volts will do), some wires with the ends stripped (a length of wire can be cut into suitable lengths of about 1 foot (30cms.) using scissors, and stripped by carefully cutting the plastic insulation about 1 inch (2 to 3 cms.) from each end and pulling it away with the blades of the scissors), a 4.5 volt bell battery, the sort with two terminals on the top and a small screwdriver.

It is not dangerous to use a 3.5v bulb with a

4.5v battery. Although it may not last quite as long as a 6v bulb, it will shine with impressive brightness.

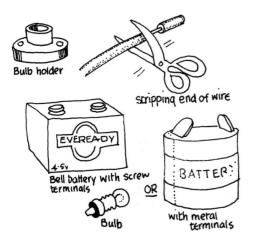

Bulb holder

stripping end of wire

EVEREADY
4·5v
Bell battery with screw terminals

OR

BATTERY
with metal terminals

Bulb

Offer a bulb in a holder with some wires and the battery to your child. Ask her to try to make the bulb light up. Be patient, it is amazing how quickly even the youngest children will succeed. Encourage her to try various ways of joining the battery to the bulb.

What she is attempting to do is to complete a circuit. You can talk in terms of making a ring of wires that come from one battery terminal, through the bulb and back to the other terminal. The diagram shows one way in which a single bulb can be made to light.

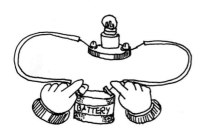

BATTERY

Two bulbs from one battery

When your child has been successful in lighting up a bulb, offer her a challenge: can she make two bulbs light up from only one battery? There are a number of ways in which this could be done so make sure that she has not only the battery, bulbs and holders, but at least half a dozen lengths of wire to choose from as well.

Once again, do not simply tell her what to do or direct her activities too closely, but allow her time to explore various possibilities.

If you feel that some clues might aid her thinking, talk about a circuit with the bulbs being part of the circle, like daisies in a chain.

There are two very distinct and very different ways of lighting two bulbs, one way will light the bulbs, but only dimly, the other will light two bulbs almost as brightly as one. The drawings show these different circuits.

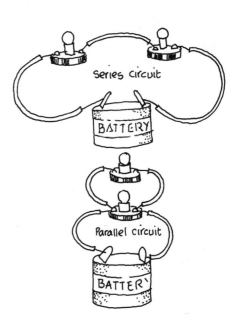

Series circuit

BATTERY

Parallel circuit

BATTERY

Making a switch

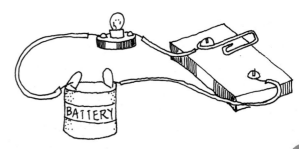

Once she has learned the simple skills of making bulbs light up your child could perhaps use these skills to add lighting to her models. A home made doll's house, a toy vehicle or a model of a light house for example would be greatly enhanced by the addition of lights. But if the circuit is made and the lights are left on for any length of time, the batteries will soon wear out. So it is useful for your child to be able to add a switch to the circuit so that the bulbs can be turned on and off whenever she wants.

She may already have noticed that if one wire coming from the battery to the bulb holder is disconnected, the bulb will go out. A switch made from a piece of wood, two drawing pins and a paper clip can be put into the circuit at this point.

An interesting investigation can be made by removing the paper clip and finding different

things to bridge the gap between the two drawing pins. Ask your child to try as many things as possible. Make one group of the things that complete the circuit and light the bulb (these are called CONDUCTORS) and another group of the things that do not allow the electrical current to flow (which are called INSULATORS – for example: rubber, wood, glass, pottery and ceramics, card, plastics etc.).

Ask her what materials the conductors are made from (they are almost invariably metals of one kind or another).

orces

MAGNETISM

Magnets can be a source of wonder and amusement for young and old alike. Magnetism, as a phenomenon, has been known for many centuries. Ancient mariners in various parts of the world used pieces of magnetic rock, called lodestone, to help them navigate. They had discovered that a piece of lodestone, suspended from a thread, always came to rest in the same position. It was then possible to shape the stone or mark it so that it indicated the direction of north. It was also discovered that steel needles could be magnetised by stroking them with the stone which could then be used to make a crude form of compass.

Good magnets are difficult to come by and can be expensive. If you are able to find a supplier, one set will give years of service if carefully looked after. However, many interesting investigations can be done using children's play magnets (often made from plastic in the shape of a horseshoe with tiny magnets attached to the ends).

Magnetic attraction

For this investigation you will need a magnet and a wide variety of simple household objects like a knife, fork and spoon, cup and saucer, pencil, rubber, tin foil, glass and plastic containers, keys, coins, paper clips and any other small objects that might be available, including nails, nuts and bolts, and needles and pins if possible.

Ask your child to hold the magnet near the fork or spoon. If we assume that it is made from steel, she will find that it is attracted to the magnet and will appear to "stick" to the magnet, requiring some effort to remove it.

Allow her time to experience and enjoy this strange effect so that she is familiar with the feel of magnetic attraction. Introduce the pile of objects and ask her to try each one in turn to discover whether or not they are also attracted to the magnet.

Ask her to make a pile of the things that are and make a separate pile of those things that are not attracted. When she has completed this task,

Forces

talk to her about the things in the two piles. What do the objects in the "attracted" pile seem to have in common. (You will probably discover that they are all metal objects, mostly made from either iron or steel.)

How strong are your magnets?

If you are fortunate to be able to get a number of magnets, this is a simple investigation that your child can do to discover which of them is the strongest.

Apart from a number of magnets, you will need a packet of paper clips or dressmaker's pins.

Ask your child to dip one end of a magnet into the box of clips or pins and to pull it out carefully and gently. She will discover that the clips form a chain hanging from the end of the magnet.

Let her count how many were attracted to the end of the magnet, then repeat the test with the other magnets. Questions for her to answer could include: which magnet picked up the most pins or clips, which one picked up the least, does one end of a magnet pick up the same number as the other end, do any stick to the middle?

Wrap it up

Does magnetic force pass through solid objects? This is one simple way for your child to find out. Have available a strong magnet, a few paper clips, a sheet of paper, a plastic bag, some cooking foil, a piece of material such as a handkerchief, a sheet of card (a piece cut from a cereal packet would be fine) and a thin book.

Ask your child to test her magnet to see if it will attract some paper clips (which it should be able to do with ease). Now ask her to wrap her magnet in a piece of paper. Will it still pick up the clips? Let her try it and see. Now ask her to wrap her magnet in each of the items in turn, the plastic, the foil and the material. Before each test ask her to guess whether or not the magnet will still be able to pick up some clips.

She should find that, even when wrapped in each of these things, the magnet is still able to attract the paper clips and pick some of them up. In fact it can be very surprising how many thicknesses of paper, plastic or foil a strong magnetic force can pass through.

Let your child try placing the clips on top of the sheet of card and then move the magnet about underneath it. The clips will be moved, as if by magic, around the surface of the card. Ask her to try it with the book too. Once she has a clip "stuck" to the book's cover using her magnet she may be able to turn the book to stand upright and move the clip up and down.

This has all sorts of possibilities for tricks and games. For example, you could help her to make a paper fly, stick it to a paper clip and make it "walk" all over a thin book, sheet of card or even a plastic tea tray, using the magnet. A magnetic fishing game is great fun. Help her to cut out small paper fish shapes and attach a clip to the nose of each one. Place the fish in a large box

and go fishing with a magnet tied to a short piece of cane with some thread.

Attracted or repelled?

This investigation requires a pair of good bar magnets, cheap play magnets, especially those made of plastic with small magnets on the ends do not work convincingly well.

The ends of a magnet are called its "poles." Many magnets are divided into two by painting one end red and the other either blue, or left bare. Alternatively, one end of the magnet will be marked with an "N" indicating the magnet's north pole.

Ask your child to place one of the magnets on a smooth surface and then to move the other magnet towards it. As the two ends get closer together one of two things will happen, either the two magnets will spring together and hold tightly or the one on the table top will attempt to slide away.

This can be felt most effectively if you hold a magnet in each hand and bring them together. Again, they will either be pulled together strongly or they will attempt to riggle away from each other. Children are especially fascinated by the latter as the magnets feel almost alive.

Get your child to take note of the way to hold them so that they attract and come together and the way in which they try to repel one another and force themselves apart. Ask her to determine whether it is when a red end touches another red end (or north pole touches north pole) that they are attracted or repelled.

You will discover that two north poles will repel as will the two south poles (the opposite ends), but a north pole will attract the south pole of another magnet very strongly.

Help her to tie or tape a magnet onto a toy car so that the magnet lies front to back. Ask her to place the vehicle on a smooth surface, like a table top, and move another magnet towards the back of it. If the car is pulled towards her magnet ask her to turn the magnet around so that the magnet on the car is repelled by the magnet in her hand.

Now every time that she brings her magnet near to the one on the car, it will be pushed away across the table top. With the second magnet taped the correct way round onto a second car, it is possible to push one at the other which will be pushed away instead of crashing heavily because of the force of magnetic repulsion.

Using the force

Once your child has discovered how to make magnets repel one another this can be used in an amusing way.

A simple compass

Get some thread, a large needle and a magnet,

Help your child to tie some thread around the centre of a magnet so that it balances well then, either hold it very still, or tie it to something suitable so that it hangs suspended in the air. The magnet will always come to rest in the same direction. If possible check that direction with a

map reading compass, the magnet like the magnetised needle in the compass will line up in the north/south position. (This is not the direction of the north pole but the position of magnetic north which lies to one side of the true pole and which alters slightly each year.)

Hang a long needle from its centre in the same way as you did the magnet. Let it come to rest then disturb it again. Try this several times and get your child to note which way it points. She will probably discover that there is no one direction in which it settles.

Now help her to stroke the needle. Always start from the same end and stroke one end of the magnet along the whole length of the needle several times. Hang the needle in the same way again and your child will discover that the needle is now acting like a compass as it has been magnetised.

SAND AND WATER CLOCKS

Measurement of time as minutes, hours, days etc., is a man-made concept based upon the movement of the earth and its passage around the sun. This is extremely difficult for a child to understand, but she becomes aware of the passing of time quite naturally by the regularity of events like meal times and bed time, night and day, birthdays, festivals and celebrations.

Learning to tell the time and remembering the names of days, months and seasons can be made into enjoyable games to play, but making her own clocks can also play an important part in developing a child's awareness of time.

The investigations that follow are designed around devices that record the passage of an arbitrary period of time. That is they are NOT made to record specific periods of seconds, minutes or hours with any accuracy, but are nonetheless very useful for timing the speed with which your child can accomplish given tasks. These are detailed for you in the text.

A simple sand clock

You will need two plastic pots like a margarine tub and a yogurt pot, some fine sand or salt, a piece of wood about 12 to 16 inches (30 to 40 cms.) long and an inch or so (2 to 3 cms.) square with another piece of wood large enough to be a base to nail the longer stick onto.

Help your child to nail the upright to the base, using a hammer and tacks. Let her Sellotape the pot to the top of the stick, having first made a small hole in the bottom with something like a nail or the point of a pair of scissors.

Encourage your child to experiment with the amount of sand or salt that she puts into the top container and the size of the hole in its base so that the sand runs out steadily and continually. Count with her, slowly and regularly, as the sand pours out to see how far she can count before the sand stops flowing.

Help her to organise her clock so that it runs steadily for about a count of 20 (although this is not critical).

Once it has been set up successfully, let your child use her timer to see how quickly she can do certain simple activities. For example, hold your finger under the pot to stop the sand from coming out while your child prepares a lace and some beads. Ask her to thread as many beads as possible while the sand is running. Release your finger as you say go, then stop her when the sand stops running and count her score. Try it again to see if she can beat her score, or change places and see how well you do with the beads.

Try the number of times she can throw up and catch a ball or run to a chair and back, the number of dried peas that can be taken (one at a time) from one pot and placed in another.

Any activity that encourages manual or bodily dexterity is worth attempting.

Water clocks

A simple water clock can be made in exactly the same way as the sand clock. Using water instead of sand, it will be necessary to help your child experiment with the hole size once more so that the water is released in a steady trickle rather than a downpour!

An interesting alternative is in the form of a shallow container with a hole in the bottom that is floated on water. The time period is that between when the container is first put in the water and when it finally sinks.

To make this form of water timer your child will need a large bowl of water and a variety of plastic pots and tubs to experiment with. Begin by helping her to make a small hole in the bottom of a margarine tub and float it in the bowl.

It is quite possible that the tub is so light that the water does not seep in. In this case suggest that your child adds some weight by putting some plasticene, marbles or stones inside so that it floats low enough in the water for the water to come through the hole.

She will need to experiment with different shaped containers, larger or smaller holes and different amounts of weight so that she ends up with a range of timers that can time quite short periods of time (approximately half a minute) to several minutes, although once again the actual period of time for each is not critical.

With your help she may discover that she has made a timer that will time a perfect boiled egg. Let her find other interesting uses for her timers as well.

MOTION

Testing toy cars

Many children collect toy cars and this is an opportunity to put such a collection to good use.

Get your child to choose four or five cars from her collection and ask her which one she thinks is the best. What does this question mean? The best looking or the most colourful perhaps, or is it the one that runs most easily and can can travel the greatest distance with one push? Discuss these various possibilities with her and ask her how she would try to discover the one that goes the furthest.

She will probably want to push the cars across a firm, level floor. Encourage her to push in the same way and equally as hard on each occasion so that one is not favoured more than another.

Which car travels the furthest? Get her to try again, does the same car go the greatest distance every time? Is there one that is always left behind?

A fairer test

Pushing the cars is open to all kinds of inaccuracies. Even when she is trying to be fair it would be impossible for your child to push equally hard every time.

One way to overcome this is to allow the cars to travel down a slope and then across the floor.

A suitable slope can be made from stiff cardboard, hardboard or even a thin metal sheet if you have one. In fact anything about 3 feet (90cms.) long, 6 inches to 1 foot (15 to 30cms.) wide and quite thin (so that there is not a noticeable step where it meets the ground) will do.

The board can be rested on a pile of books, bricks or a low stool, so that it forms a reasonable slope with the ground.

Suggest that your child puts one of her cars at the very end of the slope, then lets it go so that it can run down the slope and across the floor. Test each car again. Is the car that was judged best in the previous test still as good, and is the last still last?

Does the surface matter?

Using the slope again, ask your child to take the best car, run it down the slope once more and measure how far it goes. Get her to measure the distance using heel to toe steps, pencil lengths or even the number of cars needed to equal the distance rolled.

Now lay sheets of newspaper in front of the slope. Ask your child to repeat the test and measure again. Does the car go a greater or lesser distance this time?

Let her repeat the test on different surfaces; thick carpet, concrete path, polished tiles, crumpled paper etc. Ask her which surfaces let the car travel furthest and which seem to hold it back.

More slope less speed?

If the angle of the slope is increased, does the car go further?

Using her favourite car on a good surface let your child run her car down the slope set at a low angle. Get her to measure the distance as before.

Ask her if making the slope greater will make the car go further. Now get her to raise the slope by adding more books or bricks to the pile and to try the test again. Has the distance increased?

Let her keep raising the slope, testing at each level, until it is very steep.

She will find that, as the angle increases, so does the distance, up to a point. Beyond this point the slope is so great that the car will no longer run smoothly off the end and across the floor, but will bang into the ground and lose speed and distance.

BALLOONS

Balloon power

Blowing up balloons and watching their noisy, erratic flight around a room when you let them go is always great fun, but here is one way to harness that power.

You will need some long balloons, some straws, Sellotape and strong cotton, thin twine or nylon fishing line about the length of the room.

Help your child to push one end of the thread through a straw (using a wide straw popular in fast-food restaurants, makes this easier to do). Tie one end of the line to something suitable like the door handle or chair back at one end of the room.

Blow up the balloon and, while you hold the end tight, ask your child to use two pieces of sticky tape to join the balloon to the straw at the front and back.

Let your child take the balloon end tightly in her fingers while you stretch the line tight. When everything is ready count down together from ten and get her to release the rocket on zero. Her balloon rocket should shoot along the line for the whole length of the room.

Balloon static

Lightning is the massive discharge of static electricity that has built up in heavy rain clouds. Thunder is the sound of millions of volts of electrical power arcing between the clouds and the ground in a searing flash of light. Because sound travels many, many times slower than the speed of light, we hear the sound some seconds after the flash. Very approximately, a storm is one mile away for every 5 seconds counted between seeing the lightning and the hearing the thunder (or 1 kilometre for every 3 seconds).

The rubber skin of an inflated balloon can be charged with static electricity very easily and, although not in the least like a thunderstorm, its static charge can be made to do some interesting things.

Ask your child to slip on a woollen jumper and rub a fully inflated balloon against herself a number of times. This builds up a static charge in the skin of the balloon. Tell her to place the balloon against a wall. If she has rubbed it enough the static electricity in the balloon will cause it to "stick" against the wall as though stuck with glue. If you can reach you can even hang them from the ceiling in this way. As the charge gradually leaks away so the balloon will creep down the wall or fall from the ceiling.

Another way of showing the charge is to ask your child to hold a well rubbed balloon above her head. You can do this to one another while looking in a mirror. The static charge will attract fine hair and make her look as if her hair is standing on end. (This can also be done by combing her hair with a plastic comb a number of times, to build up a charge, and then holding it above her hair.)

A balloon or a comb, well rubbed once more, can also be held over tiny scraps of tissue paper which are attracted to the balloon or comb almost as if they were magnetised.

Balloon music!

Experiments in sound show that musical sounds can be generated by making things shake or vibrate like the skin of a drum being banged, the strings of a guitar being plucked or the reed of a clarinet being blown.

The neck of a balloon can be made to vibrate by blowing up the balloon and then pulling the neck into a narrow slit using the finger and thumb of both hands to pull either side of the opening.

Let your child experiment with the sounds by pulling harder or more gently.

The sounds that she will get from her balloon are hardly musical but the vibrations can be clearly felt. This is also true if you hold a fully inflated balloon between you and sing or speak against the skin of the balloon. If one of you sings, the other should lightly touch the balloon to feel the vibrations of the sounds.

Another way to make the balloon skin vibrate is to pull it over the end of a cardboard tube. Help your child to stretch it very tightly across the end of a long card tube. It can be secured with some sticky tape. If you have enough balloons to spare this can be repeated using tubes of different lengths. (The cardboard tubes from packs of tin foil are very good for this purpose.) When the drums are tapped or banged using fingers or a spoon handle or a piece of wood, the different lengths of drum give different pitched notes.

FINDING THE BALANCE POINT

We use scales in so many different ways almost every week of our lives. Bathroom scales, to tell us the worst, or kitchen scales to help us prepare our meals, scales in shops to weigh our purchases and even at the bank to weigh bags of coins.

Helping children to understand balance and how scales may be made and used is an important activity that can be done very simply.

Yogurt pot scales

For this activity your child will need a garden cane, or a similar shaped piece of wood about 16 to 20 inches (40 to 60cms.) long, some strong thread or twine, two identical, large, plastic pots and some weights such as marbles, small stones, conkers or play bricks.

Help her to make three holes in the rim of each pot, evenly spaced around the edges, using the point of a pair of scissors or a large needle. Get her to tie a piece of thread about 4 inches (10cms.) long to each of the holes and help her to tie them together above the pot so that they can be hung from each end of the cane, securing them in place with a piece of sticky tape.

Help her to loosely tie another piece of string or twine to the centre of the cane so that the balance can be lifted by it. Get her to move the string towards one end or the other to make her scales balance straight and level. She will find that moving the string towards the end that is drooping down will help to bring it into line.

When the exact balance point has been found, tie the string tightly and secure it with tape.

The central string can either be held or, more conveniently, can be tied to anything that will allow the balance to be suspended at a reasonable height for your child to use.

Using the scales

Get her to check that her scales are balanced properly, fine adjustments can be made by putting a tiny piece of plasticene on the lighter, higher end.

Ask her to discover how many marbles (or conkers, or stones, or play bricks) it takes to exactly balance her favourite small toy, or an apple, or an egg.

As an alternative to this, give your child a ball of plasticene and ask her to divide it into two pieces. Tell her to use her balance to see if they weigh the same amount. If she puts one piece in one pot and the other piece in the second pot she will discover that she will have to remove some plasticene from the heavier, lower pot and add it to the lighter, higher pot until her balance is level.

Seesaws . . .

Seesaws are to be found in many playgrounds and, although they can be a great source of fun and enjoyment, so much can be learned from them too.

If your child is playing with a friend on a seesaw, ask them to sit very still to see if they balance. It is quite likely that one will be a little heavier than the other and the seesaw won't balance exactly. Ask them to try to find a way of adjusting the balance simply by moving their weight nearer or further from the centre.

They will quickly discover that if the heavier child moves nearer the centre and the lighter child moves as far back along the beam as possible it will help to achieve a better balance.

In fact a young child at the very end of one side of the seesaw can balance the weight of an adult so long as the adult sits very close to the central pivot.

. . and mobiles

he art of making an interesting mobile is to be
ble to balance a large, heavy shape with a much
maller cluster of shapes.

For this your child will need four to six lengths
f thin garden cane (thin split cane used for
upporting small potted house plants is perfect,
ternatively, lengths cut from wire coat hangers
sing a strong pair of pliers are just as good). She
ill also need a reel of cotton, stiff paper or thin
ard and coloured pens and pencils or paints to
raw and decorate her shapes and a pair of
issors to cut them out.

First help her to plan the theme for the
obile. She may choose a sky scene with sun,
ouds, birds or planes; a night scene with stars,
oon, comets and rockets; a teddy bears' picnic
ith teddies, trees, cakes and jellies, the
ossibilities are endless.

Help her to draw and colour a variety of
shapes and attach each to a length of cotton.

Begin by loosely tying a length of cotton to
the centre of one of the canes. Ask your child to
move the thread until the cane exactly balances.
Now ask her to tie one large shape to one end of
the cane and a smaller one to the other end.
When it is lifted by the central thread it no longer
balances. Ask her again to move the central
thread to make the cane balance straight and
level once more.

Experience from the seesaw problem may
help her to see that if the central thread is moved
away from the smaller, lighter shape and
towards the larger, heavier one the mobile can
be made to balance.

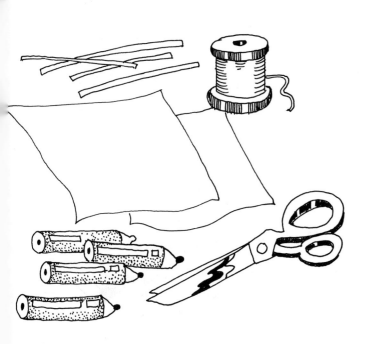

A more complex mobile can be made by adding other canes and further shapes. Your child will need to rebalance it at each stage by moving the supporting strings. When it is finally completed the strings should be tied tightly and fixed in position with a little sticky tape. The final effect will be well worth the effort.